3

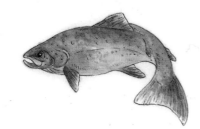

Salmon

In memory of Lauren, who had the kindest soul and
a particular fondness for ferrets.
A.L. x

For Papa Bear and Louis Bear.
K.P.

First published in 2022 by Boxer Books Limited.
www.boxerbooks.com
Boxer® is a registered trademark of Boxer Books Limited.
Text copyright © 2022 Alison Limentani
Illustrations copyright © 2022 Katie Putt

The right of Alison Limentani to be identified as the author and Katie Putt
as the illustrator of this work has been asserted by them in accordance with
the Copyright, Designs and Patents Act, 1988.

ISBN 978-1-912757-97-8

1 3 5 7 9 10 8 6 4 2

Printed in China

All of our papers are sourced from managed forests and renewable resources.

Ferret

Bighorn Sheep

Nature's Treasures of
NORTH AMERICA

Nine-banded
Armadillo

Written by Alison Limentani   Illustrated by Katie Putt

Boxer Books

Contents

Bison

NORTH AMERICA

This map of North America includes the USA and Canada.

Atlantic Ocean

Pacific Ocean

Rocky Mountains

Yellowstone

Yosemite

Grand Canyon

Sonoran Desert

Everglades

7

Woodland and Forests

Woodland and forests are places where lots of trees grow together. North American woodlands are filled with evergreen trees like pines, firs, and spruce trees. These are trees that stay green all year round — ever green!

Did you know about a third of North America is woodland?

Redwood trees can live for more than 2,000 years and reach more than 305 feet high! That's as tall as the Statue of Liberty.

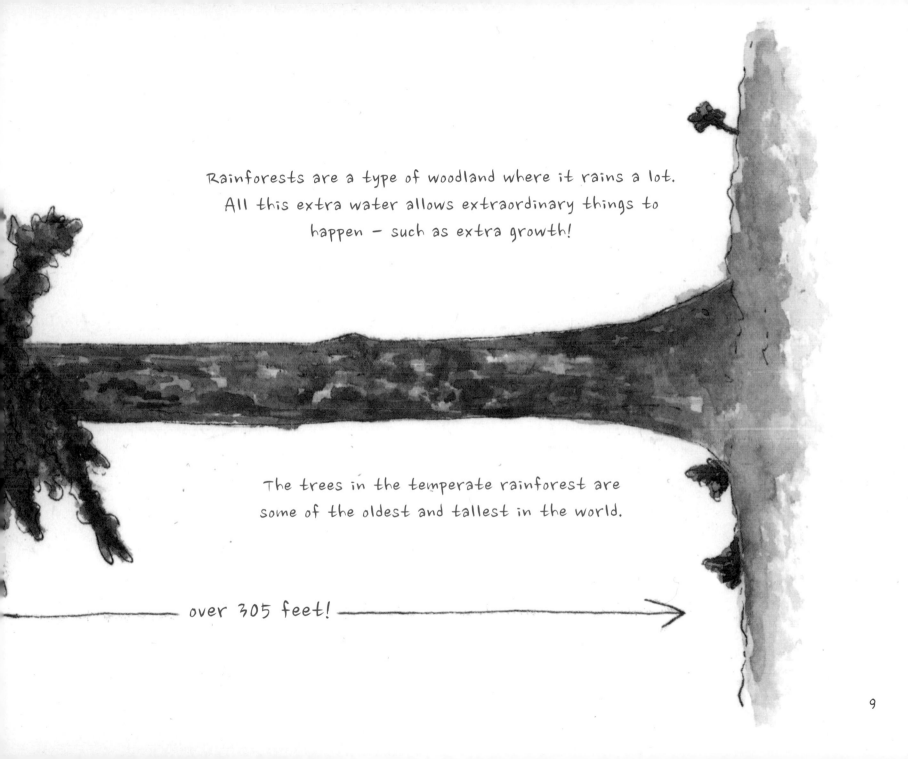

Rainforests are a type of woodland where it rains a lot.
All this extra water allows extraordinary things to
happen — such as extra growth!

The trees in the temperate rainforest are
some of the oldest and tallest in the world.

over 305 feet!

All sorts of birds make their homes high up in the trees.

Steller's Jay

The Steller's jay is a bright blue bird with a crest of feathers on its head.

Woodpecker

Woodpeckers have extra-long tongues to catch the tasty grubs they uncover by pecking holes in the trees.

Northern Spotted Owl

The Northern spotted Owl is a brown owl with dark eyes. They sleep during the day and come out at night to hunt. They talk to each other in hoots, whistles, and barks.

Pacific Fisher

Pacific fishers are excellent tree climbers.
Their sharp claws help them grip onto branches.
They have beautifully soft fur that is darker
in the winter than it is in the summer.

They live inside the hollows of
old trees, coming out at dusk
and dawn to hunt for food.

Raccoon

Raccoons are very cheeky! They like to raid people's garbage and will eat almost anything, but they prefer to dunk it in water first.

Nine-banded Armadillo

Nine-banded armadillos have a hard, armored shell and very tough skin. They hide from other animals by curling up.

Bobcat

Bobcats are double the size of pet cats and have thick, spotty fur.

Pacific Coast

Along the Pacific coast the beaches are lined with cliffs and rocky outcrops. Tall sea stacks tower out of the water. They were made by the crashing ocean wearing away the rock around them, leaving them standing alone in the water.

Tufted Puffin

Tufted puffins make their homes in shallow burrows high up on the sea stacks.

Sealion

Enormous sealions may look clumsy on land, but in the water their strong flippers help them swim at speeds of up to 35 miles per hour.

Sea Stars

Brightly colored sea stars use tiny
suckers on their arms to help them
cling to rocks or creep slowly across
the sea floor.

Pelican

Pelicans have a stretchy pouch in their
mouths. They dive head-first into the
sea with their mouths open wide, ready
to fill it with fish.

Fjords and Waterfalls

Fjords are long, narrow strips of water, with three very steep sides, leading to the sea. They were created by large chunks of ice melting and often have waterfalls.

Each summer, huge numbers of salmon start their long journey from the sea, up rivers to get back to the place they were born. They travel hundreds of miles. They struggle against the current and even have to jump up rapids and small waterfalls.

Brown Bears

Hungry brown bears wait at the top of the falls to grab the fish as they fly through the air.

The bears eat a lot of fish to make sure they have enough fat stores to sleep through the cold winter months.

Did you know that the skin of the salmon turns bright red as it gets closer to its destination?

— Waterways

Thousands of rivers, lakes, and bogs are dotted throughout the North American woodlands, making perfect homes for animals that love water.

Beavers

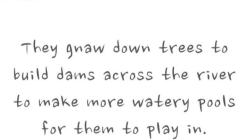

They gnaw down trees to build dams across the river to make more watery pools for them to play in.

Beavers have waterproof fur and a big flat scaly tail to help them swim through the water.

River Otter

River otters can hold their breath underwater for about eight minutes.

Moose

Moose feed on plants growing in the lakes and bogs. They are huge animals and can be recognized by their unusual-shaped antlers and droopy nose.

Mangroves

The Everglades are an incredible tropical wetland where mangrove forests grow out of the water on tall stilt-like roots.

Manatee

Manatees graze on plants growing underneath the water, like huge swimming 'sea cows'.

Marsh Rabbit

Floating Pennywort

Marsh rabbits swim through the shallow waters looking for floating plants, like pennywort, to munch on.

Mangrove Trees

Alligator

Scaly alligators float in the water like submerged logs, but don't be fooled! With about 80 sharp teeth in their mouths, you do not want to get bitten!

Coral Reefs

The coral reef in Florida is one of the biggest in the world. The colorful underwater landscape is created by strange plant-like animals that aren't able to move around the ocean. These corals and sponges come in lots of different shapes and colors. Some are even shaped like elk horns!

Loggerhead Sea Turtle

Elkhorn Coral

Loggerhead sea turtles fly through the water, flapping their front flippers like wings, and using their back flippers to steer them like the rudder of a ship.

Angelfish

Colourful angelfish hide among the coral. They get their name from their large fins, which are shaped like angel wings. There are lots of different types of angelfish in all sorts of colours.

Parrot Fish

Rainbow parrot fish are multicoloured fish with beak-like mouths. They move through the reef in groups known as schools, grazing on the algae that grow on the corals. Algae are simple plants that live in water, but do not flower.

 # Mountains

Mountains are very big rocky hills that range across vast areas of North America. Some mountains, like the Rockies, have pine forests running across their rugged landscape. Watch out: now we're in mountain lion territory.

Mountain lions

Mountain lions are powerful orange cats that like to catch their dinner by jumping down on it from above.

24

Ringtail

Ringtails use their striped tail for balance as they dash through trees and shrubs and over rocks.

Bighorn Sheep

Bighorn sheep have big curved horns on their heads. They are brilliant at climbing and jumping over rocks.

Mountain Goat

Mountain goats have fluffy
white coats. They skip across
steep mountainsides that
look almost impossible
to cross.

Great Plains

The great plains are large areas of prairie land where lots of long grasses grow. Grazing animals are attracted to the great plains by the lush grass that they can eat.

Chicory

Buttercup

Sunflower

Blazing Star

All sorts of wildflowers grow among the grasses, from the bright yellow flowers of sunflowers and buttercups, to the gentle purple petals of chicory and blazing star flowers.

Prairie Dogs

Prairie dogs are not actually dogs at all, but ground squirrels. Rather than living up in the trees, prairie dogs live underground in a network of burrows. The burrows help to keep the grass green by catching the rainwater. Without them, the rainwater would run off into rivers.

Bison

Bison are giant cow-like animals that have big humps on their backs, horns, and a fluffy hair-do.

Pronghorn

Pronghorns graze in herds. They can move faster than 50 miles per hour when they need to outrun bobcats or coyotes – that's almost as fast as the school bus!

Ferret

Black-footed ferrets are very playful.
They like to arch their long backs and
dance about on their short little legs
before wrestling each other.

Skunk

When they are scared, striped skunks arch
their backs and stamp their feet. This means
they are about to squirt disgusting smelly liquid
from their bottoms. Quick! Step back!

Arctic Tundra

The Arctic tundra is a very cold place. The frozen ground makes it difficult for plants to take root in the soil. No trees grow here. Arctic hares graze on small shrubs and grasses grown during the short summer months.

Snow Geese

Flocks of snow geese fly south for the winter to holiday along the warmer southern coast. You can often hear them honking loudly as they fly over in a 'V' formation.

Arctic Fox

Arctic foxes are white to help camouflage them against the snowy landscape.

Arctic Hare

Arctic hares have a brilliant sense of smell to help them find plants growing beneath the snow.

Desert

Can you imagine what it's like to live in a desert? Deserts are places where there is very little rain, so the plants and animals have special ways to survive without water. Cacti can store lots of water inside their fat stems. They have prickles all over to protect them from thirsty animals.

Deserts are a good place to find reptiles because they are cold blooded.

Desert Iguana

This means their body temperature changes depending on how hot or cold it is outside.

Desert iguanas need the heat of the desert to get moving. When they get cold, they move very slowly and have to spend a lot of time basking in the sun to warm up.

Kangaroo Rat

Desert animals like the kangaroo rat are nocturnal and only come out at night. This helps them avoid the hottest times of day.

Desert Tortoise

Kit Fox

Kit foxes dig themselves dens to hide in.

Some animals spend time in underground burrows to escape the heat of the desert. When things get too hot, desert tortoises will dig themselves into the ground to escape the heat. They can hibernate in their burrows for months at a time if they need to.

35

The Sonoran desert is one of North America's hottest deserts and home to the Saguaro Cactus. The cactus feeds the desert animals, but it needs special help from bats and birds to pollinate its flowers before it can make them into fruit.

Cactus

Pollination is when an animal rubs pollen from one part of the flower onto another. White flowers that smell of ripe melons grow at the top of the cactus stem.

Bat Pollinating

The smell attracts birds, bees and bats to come and feed. When these animals push their heads into the flower, they actually pollinate the plant!

Once the plant is pollinated it produces bright red fruits below the white flowers. These fruits contain about 2,000 small black seeds. When the fruit is ripe, it splits open and birds, bats, javelina, coyotes and tortoises all feed on it.

White-winged Dove

Javelina

Fruit

The animals then take the seeds across the desert in their poo so more cacti can grow!

Javelina are hairy boar-like animals with short legs, a pig-like nose and long, brown fur.

National Parks

The people of North America think that some of nature's treasures are so special that they need to be looked after. These 'protected' areas are called National Parks.

Black Bear

Black bears prefer to live in forests, where they can hide among the trees and use the leaves for bedding.

There are 63 National Parks in North America. Yosemite is one of them.

Yosemite has giant forests and deep rocky valleys with some of the tallest waterfalls in the world. Yosemite Falls is almost as tall as two Empire State buildings stacked on top of each other!

Yellowstone was the first ever National Park. It follows the Yellowstone river and is famous for its waterfalls, mountains, and colorful hot springs. It is home to bison, bald eagles, brown bears, wolves, and elk.

Male elk grow huge antlers each year.

Elk

Imagine how heavy it must be carrying those antlers around on your head!

Bald eagles fly high in the skies. They like to catch fish in the river. The bald eagle is the national symbol of the USA.

Bald Eagle

Wolf

For a while there were no wolves in Yellowstone Park. People thought the park would be a better place without them, so they removed them. Wolves eat the elk, but without them the elk took over. They ate everything, so there were no plants left for the other animals. Luckily, scientists realized what was happening and brought the wolves back, so now there is enough food for everyone.

The Grand Canyon is a deep hole carved into red rock by the Colorado River. It is really big: more than 220 miles long and nearly a mile deep! That's almost as deep as three One World Trade Centers are high! Large parts of the Grand Canyon are dry like deserts and rocky like mountains. There are lots of hiking trails around this National Park.

Coyote

Greater roadrunners are very fast birds. They use their speed to chase after lizards and snakes.

Coyotes live around the Grand Canyon, along with lots of other creatures. They look a bit like dogs and are related to wolves.

Greater Roadrunner

Rattlesnake

Rattlesnakes have a special rattle at the ends of their tails. They shake it to make a loud noise that scares off animals that come too close.

Bark Scorpion

Babies

Bark scorpions have big pincers and a poisonous sting in their tails, but they can be very caring too.
A mother will carry up to 30 babies around on her back until they are old enough to look after themselves.

Index

Buttercup

Woodpecker

Prairie Dogs

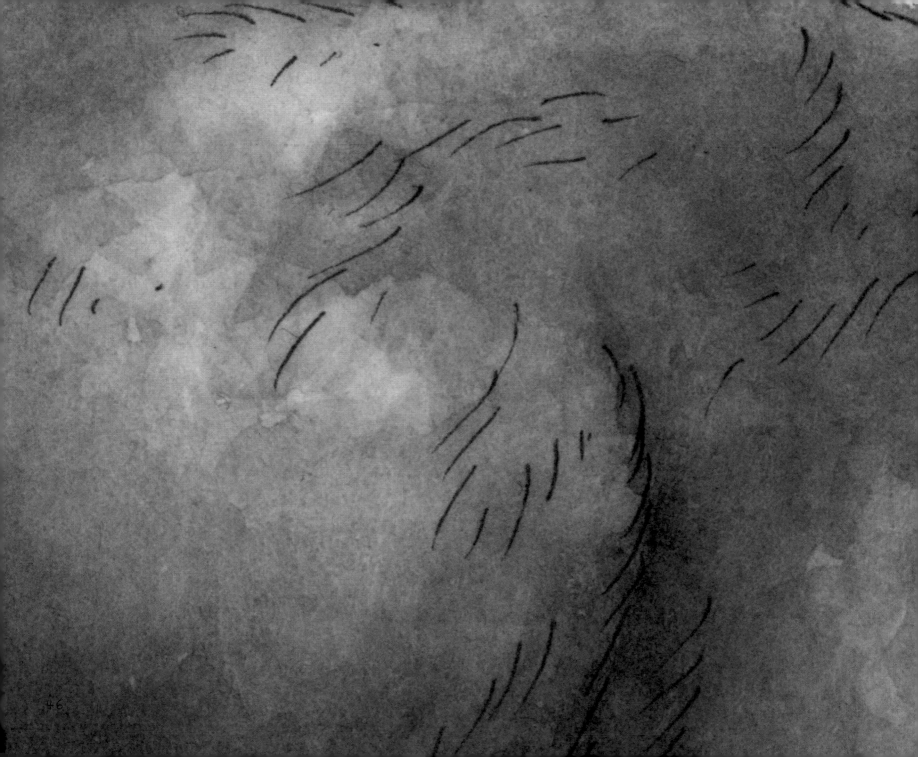